21ST
Century
Skills Library

REAL WORLD MATH: HEALTH AND WELLNESS

GARDENING BY THE NUMBERS

Cecilia Minden

Cherry Lake Publishing
Ann Arbor, Michigan

Published in the United States of America by Cherry Lake Publishing
Ann Arbor, MI
www.cherrylakepublishing.com

Math Adviser: Tonya Walker, MA, Boston University

Nutrition Adviser: Steven Abrams, MD, Professor of Pediatrics, Baylor College of Medicine, Houston, Texas

Photo Credits: Page 14, © Randy Faris/Corbis

Library of Congress Cataloging-in-Publication Data
Minden, Cecilia.
 Gardening by the numbers / by Cecilia Minden.
    p. cm. — (Real world math)
 ISBN-13: 978-1-60279-008-7
 ISBN-10: 1-60279-008-6
 1. Vegetable gardening—Juvenile literature. 2. Fruit-culture—Juvenile literature. 3. Arithmetic—Juvenile literature. I. Title. II. Series.

 SB324.M54 2008
 635—dc22   2007005414

Cherry Lake Publishing would like to acknowledge the work of
The Partnership for 21st Century Skills.
Please visit www.21stcenturyskills.org for more information.

TABLE OF CONTENTS

CHAPTER ONE

BE A FARMER!

*A fruit-and-vegetable stand or farmer's market
can be a great place to buy fresh produce.*

There's nothing quite like a colorful, crisp salad or a bowl brimming

with sweet berries. Where does your family buy its **produce**? Maybe you

shop at a local market or drive to a favorite fruit-and-vegetable stand. Or maybe you don't even have to leave your backyard. It's possible to grow your own produce in a garden at home!

Gardening is a great way to get fresh fruits and vegetables. It can be relatively quick and easy if you follow directions, use your math skills, and remain organized. You simply need to be sure to plant and follow the instructions on the seed packet. Then keep an eye on the plants as they develop. As a bonus, working outdoors and staying busy will also give you a chance to exercise and relieve stress.

There's another bonus to having a garden full of fresh produce. You have more control over what is used to help plants grow and keep bugs away. Large farms often use **fertilizers** or **pesticides**, but you don't have to.

Planting a garden takes planning and research. A friend or relative who gardens can help you. Your local public library has many books on gardening. Workers at a nearby farm or **greenhouse** might also be excellent sources of information. You also should think carefully about what you want to grow. How much space do you have? Do you have the time to dedicate to certain plants that might require more care? Will you eat all the produce that some plants **yield**? One tomato plant may produce more than 50 tomatoes!

Try to make sure that your garden includes a variety of fruits and vegetables. That way, you will receive the largest sampling of **nutrients** that your body needs to grow. Raising colorful produce will also make your garden more interesting. Get creative! Imagine that your garden is supposed to look like a box of crayons. Blueberries, pumpkins, tomatoes, beans, carrots, and squash are just a few selections that can brighten your yard and provide excellent nutritional value.

REAL WORLD MATH CHALLENGE

Alejandro wants to be certain that his fruit and vegetable garden is as colorful as possible. He makes a list of plants (and colors) that might make nice additions. **Assuming Alejandro wants to include one orange fruit or vegetable, one green fruit or vegetable, and one red fruit or vegetable, how many combinations would he be able to create based on the list below?**

Orange: carrots, pumpkins, sweet potatoes

Green: spinach, green peppers, green beans

Red: tomatoes, strawberries, radishes

(Turn to page 29 for the answer)

21st Century Content

Check out www. MyPyramid.gov to learn about the different food groups and how much you should eat from each group every day. Experts say that a 9- to 13-year-old needs about 2 to 2.5 cups of vegetables and 1.5 cups of fruit on a daily basis.

A greenhouse has many different flower and vegetable plants for sale. The people who work there can be a good source of gardening information.

CHAPTER TWO

GETTING STARTED

*You will probably want a good pair of gardening gloves
to wear when you are working in your garden.*

After you consider what kinds of seeds to plant, you'll need to pick the

best location for your garden. This will affect how well your plants grow.

Most vegetables and fruits require six to eight hours of sunlight every day to develop. Look for areas in your yard or along your house or apartment building that receive plenty of natural light.

REAL WORLD MATH CHALLENGE

Katie is searching for the best spot to plant her tomato plants. The east side of her house gets 6 hours and 45 minutes of sunlight each day. The west side receives 7 hours and 15 minutes of sunlight on a daily basis. **How much less sunlight does the east side receive?** Keep in mind that there are 60 minutes in 1 hour.

(Turn to page 29 for the answer)

Now it is time to gather your gardening supplies. Items that come in handy include a shovel, gardening gloves, and a watering can or garden hose. Don't forget a garden hat and sunscreen to protect you from the sun. Many people often purchase fertilizers to aid in plant development. They might also purchase sprays to get rid of weeds and certain insects. If you're worried about larger animals such as deer or rabbits eating your produce, consider buying plastic netting to cover your plants.

After you choose the location for your garden,
you will need to prepare the soil.

After you've collected your supplies, set the **perimeters** of your garden.

Dig up the soil to a depth of 8 to 10 inches (20 to 25 centimeters). Make

sure the soil slopes slightly to provide good **drainage**. Then mark straight

rows 12 to 18 inches (30 to 46 cm) apart. How deep you dig and the

number of rows you mark will depend on how much space you have and

the type and amount of seeds you are planting. Most seed packages have

specific instructions to guide you. It is a good idea to talk to a gardening

expert before you begin working the soil.

You might choose to use seedlings. Seedlings are baby plants that already

have leaves. Seedlings cost a little more but are already partially developed.

Using seedlings can sometimes reduce growing time by weeks. Carefully

review any directions that come with the seedlings regarding planting, light

requirements, watering, and how long it takes for them to completely develop.

Keep track of this information as you plant and begin the day-to-day care of your garden. Writing in a garden notebook or journal might help you stay organized. It can provide a record of what you planted and when you planted it. You can also use the notebook to keep track of the last time you watered or used fertilizer and when you can expect to pick your fruits and vegetables.

Gardening involves many responsibilities. A little organization and strong math skills will help you get the work done. The end result is delicious and nutritious produce. Do you have your journal and a calculator handy? It's time to plant some seeds!

CHAPTER THREE

DO THE MATH: TIME TO GROW

It is exciting to see your plants begin to grow!

Most plants need sun, soil, nutrients, and water. Each kind of plant has

very specific requirements for the best possible growth. If you are a new

gardener, consider starting with two or three easy-to-grow plants, such as

Make sure you give your plants the right amount of water.

lettuce, spinach, or radishes. You can add other fruits and vegetables as you

gain experience with gardening.

No matter what you choose to plant, however, don't forget to use that

garden notebook! Your journal might prove especially helpful in recording weather information. Weather affects your plants' growth. For example, if there's just been a big rainstorm, you may not need to water for a few days. On the other hand, if the weather is hot and dry, you need to give your garden more water.

REAL WORLD MATH CHALLENGE

Nadia is growing tomatoes this summer. They need about 2 inches (5 cm) of water each week. She collected data for the month of June to see if her plants were getting enough water. When her sprinkler system runs for 15 minutes, it provides about 1 inch (2.5 cm) of water. Nadia made the following entries in her gardening journal:

Week 1: I ran the sprinkler system for a total of 30 minutes this week

Week 2: We received 1 inch (2.5 cm) of rain, and I ran the sprinkler system for 15 minutes.

Week 3: I ran the sprinkler system for 15 minutes. Later on, we received 2 inches (5 cm) of rain.

Week 4: We received 0.5 inch (1.3 cm) of rain, and I ran the sprinkler system for 15 minutes.

How much water do Nadia's tomatoes need for the entire month? Keep in mind that there are about 4 weeks in 1 month.

How much water did Nadia's tomatoes receive in June?

Did they receive enough water for the entire month?

(Turn to page 29 for the answers)

Grapes grow well in places that are warm year-round, such as California.

Don't forget that certain fruits and vegetables grow best in certain

climates. Some fruits thrive in areas that are warm year-round. Grapes

grow well in parts of California. Cauliflower, lettuce, spinach, potatoes,

21st CENTURY SKILLS LIBRARY

and onions do well in cooler climates. Ask local gardeners for ideas on

choosing the right produce to grow in your area. They can suggest the best

seeds, fertilizers, and planting times. They can also advise you on watering

requirements and what adjustments might need to be made.

REAL WORLD MATH CHALLENGE

Larry decides to plant pumpkins in this year's garden. He wants to **harvest** them by October 1 so he can use them to decorate his house for autumn and Halloween. After talking to an expert at the local greenhouse, Larry learns that pumpkin seeds usually take about 100 days to fully develop into fruit. He flips through the pages of a calendar and guesses that he'll need to plant sometime in June. He notes that there are 30 days in September, 31 days in August, 31 days in July, and 30 days in June.

If Larry plants on June 1, will that give the seeds enough time to mature? Is there a different date that Larry should plan to plant?

(Turn to page 29 for the answers)

CHAPTER FOUR

DO THE MATH: TIME TO HARVEST

School calendars in many places were planned to give students time off to help their families with planting and harvesting.

Did you know that in many places, school years were originally planned around gardening and farming? Students in farm communities were needed to help with planting and harvesting. Families planted seeds in the spring and harvested crops before the first frost hit in the fall. So schools didn't hold classes during those times.

The same growing schedule continues to be used today. Planting still occurs in spring after the last frost. This is usually in April or May for a vegetable garden. Write down the planting date for each crop in your garden notebook. You can estimate from that date when to harvest, based on how much time each type of plant normally takes to fully develop.

REAL WORLD MATH CHALLENGE

Esther is attempting to grow 15 lettuce plants in her garden. She plants 5 seeds on July 1, 5 seeds on July 6, and the final 5 seeds on July 9. The first 5 lettuce plants are ready to harvest on July 22—the exact date Esther planned for in her garden journal! **Based on this harvest date, how long does it take lettuce plants to fully mature from seeds?**

What percentage of Esther's lettuce plants was ready to harvest on July 22?

What percentage was not ready?

When is it likely that the other lettuce plants will be ready to harvest?

(Turn to page 29 for the answers)

21st Century Content

Harvest festivals are celebrated all over the world. They are often part of religious beliefs or customs. *Lunasa* is an old Irish word meaning "August." Irish people celebrate Lunasa with picnics and fairs. The Yam Festival is celebrated at the end of the rainy season in Africa. In China, people eat moon cakes to celebrate the Harvest Moon Festival.

Unexpected cool weather that causes frost can kill growing plants.

Despite your best guesses, however, you can't always pick an exact date for your harvest. Many factors will affect the growth of each crop. Some of these are out of your control. Factors might include temperature, amount of rainfall, and amount of sunlight as seeds grew and matured. How regularly you watered and (possibly) added fertilizer affect growth as well. Perhaps there were unexpected freezing temperatures in early April. Cooler weather, especially when it is cold enough to freeze moisture, can kill growing plants. Maybe the last few weeks of May featured several cloudy days, and your plants didn't get as much sunlight as expected. As a result, it may take a little extra time before they're ready to harvest.

The best way to keep track of rain in your garden is a rain gauge. A rain gauge catches rain as it is falling and allows you to measure the total amount of water that has dropped to the ground. This gives you a good idea of how much rain your crops have received. Record the amounts measured in your rain gauge in your garden journal. Are the measurements less than what your plants need to grow? Then it is time to grab your watering can or turn on your sprinkler system!

If you observe extreme changes in sunlight, rainfall, or temperatures, note these in your journal, too. You might not be able to predict a precise harvest date. But this information will keep you from being too surprised if your vegetables and fruits aren't ready for the dinner table in the time you originally estimated!

REAL WORLD MATH CHALLENGE

Ian is disappointed when he sees his potatoes aren't ready to harvest by July 17— the date he predicted in his journal. He planted on March 29, and a local gardener told him it would take about 110 days before the potatoes were fully developed. Ian looks back in his journal and sees that he made quite a few notes in April and May about several rainy days. He didn't have a rain gauge at the time, so he continued to water his plants regularly. Unfortunately, too much water can damage potato crops. Luckily, some potatoes are finally ready to harvest on July 29.

How long did it take for these vegetables to fully mature?

(Turn to page 29 for the answer)

CHAPTER FIVE

ENJOYING THE YIELD

Freshly picked strawberries are a delicious treat!

Fruits and vegetables give clues that let you know they are ready to

harvest. It is easy to see when an apple is ripe or strawberries need picking.

Other crops may require a bit more research on your part. **Corn silks**, for example, turn brown and dry when corn is ready to be harvested. Peanuts need to be pulled up just before the first hard frost. Pick beans before the seeds show their shape through the pod.

Eat corn on the cob immediately after harvesting for the best flavor.

Some of the produce you harvest will last for weeks or even months if stored in a dark, cool place. Apples can be kept for a month in your refrigerator. Other fruits should be eaten or frozen within a week of being picked. Vegetables vary. Many people think corn on the cob is best when eaten immediately after a harvest. Some corn growers even put a pot of water on to boil before they go outside to gather up their yield! Other vegetables will last three to seven days in your refrigerator.

REAL WORLD MATH CHALLENGE

Hailey harvests 19 apples from a tree in her garden and stores them in her refrigerator. She eats 6 apples the first week, 5 the second week, 3 the third week, and 2 the fourth week.

How many apples has Hailey eaten by the end of the fourth week?

How many apples are still left in the refrigerator?

Keeping in mind that these fruits can be kept in the refrigerator for about a month, how much longer can Hailey store the remaining apples?

(Remember, there are 7 days in a week and about 30 days in a month.)

(Turn to page 29 for the answers)

The harvest is in. What are you going to do with all your produce?

You can share it with friends or sell it at a local farmers' market. Are

you interested in saving the food so your family can use it later? Ask an

If you grow more vegetables than you can eat, you can sell them at a farmer's market or share them with friends and neighbors.

Learning how to preserve your fruits and vegetables will let you enjoy your harvest long after the growing season ends.

In 1999, Gerry Checkon of Altoona, Pennsylvania, grew a 1,131-pound (513-kilogram) pumpkin. According to the 1996 *Guinness Book of World Records*, the world's largest watermelon weighed 262 pounds (119 kg). What do you think you need to do if you want to grow giant vegetables?

If you want to grow giant vegetables, you need to pay careful attention to the quality of the soil and the quality of the seeds you plant. You also need to constantly monitor growing conditions and be willing to adjust your methods as necessary. A good gardener understands the way all of these factors work together to produce the best fruits and vegetables.

experienced cook or gardener about the best methods of **preserving**

various fruits and vegetables.

Gardening is a rewarding experience. Your math skills will grow along

with your plants. Another important benefit is that the produce you raise

is filled with nutrients that you and everyone in your family need for good

health. So have you decided what you'll grow in your garden yet?

Planting a garden is fun and can help your math skills grow.

REAL WORLD MATH CHALLENGE ANSWERS

Chapter One
Page 7

Alejandro can create 27 different combinations that include one orange, one green, and one red fruit or vegetable.

3 x 3 x 3 = 27

Chapter Two
Page 9

The east side of Katie's house gets 30 minutes less sunlight per day than the west side of her house.

6 x 60 minutes = 360 minutes + 45 minutes = 405 total minutes of sunlight per day on the east side

7 x 60 minutes = 420 minutes + 15 minutes = 435 total minutes of sunlight on the west side

435 − 405 = 30 minutes less sunlight per day on the east side of the house

Chapter Three
Page 15

Nadia's tomatoes need about 8 inches (20 cm) of water per month.

4 x 2 inches = 8 inches

The tomatoes received 8.5 inches (22 cm) of water in June.

2 inches + 2 inches + 3 inches + 1.5 inches = 8.5 inches

The tomatoes received about 0.5 inch (1.3 cm) more water than they needed.

8.5 inches − 8 inches = 0.5 inch

Page 17

If Larry plants the seeds on June 1 and wants to harvest on October 1, that gives the pumpkins 122 days to mature.

30 days + 31 days + 31 days + 30 days = 122 days

Pumpkins usually mature in about 100 days, so that is about 22 days longer than he needs to grow them.

122 days − 100 days = 22 days

It would be better if Larry planted the seeds 22 days later, on June 23.

1 + 22 = 23

Chapter Four
Page 19

It take lettuce plants 21 days to fully mature from seeds.

22 − 1 = 21 days

33 percent of the plants were ready to harvest on July 22.

5 ÷ 15 = 0.33 = 33%

67 percent of the plants were not ready to harvest by July 22.

100% − 33% = 67%

The lettuce plants that were planted on July 6 should be ready to harvest on July 27.

6 + 21 = 27

The lettuce plants that were planted on July 9 should be ready to harvest on July 30.

9 + 21 = 30

Page 22

Ian's potato crop took 12 days longer to be ready to harvest than he originally predicted.

29 − 17 = 12 days

It took a total of 122 days for his potato crop to fully mature.

110 days + 12 days = 122 days

Chapter Five
Page 25

Hailey has eaten 16 apples by the end of the fourth week.

6 apples + 5 apples + 3 apples + 2 apples = 16 apples

There are 3 apples left in the refrigerator.

19 apples − 16 apples = 3 apples

Hailey has about 2 days left to store the apples in the refrigerator.

7 days in a week x 4 weeks = 28 days

30 days − 28 days = 2 days

GLOSSARY

corn silks (KORN SILKS) long strands protruding from the end of a corncob

drainage (DRAY-nij) the act of carrying away surface water

fertilizers (FUR-tuhl-eyz-urz) substances used to treat soil to improve plant growth

greenhouse (GREEN-house) a structure in which the temperature and amount of light are regulated to help plants grow

harvest (HAR-vihst) to gather or collect a crop

nutrients (NU-tree-uhnts) ingredients in food that provide nourishment

perimeters (puh-RIH-muh-turz) boundaries or outer limits

pesticides (PES-tuh-sydz) chemicals used to repel or destroy certain insects

preserving (pri-ZURV-ing) storing a food product in a can or jar for future use

produce (PRO-doos) fresh fruits or vegetables that are grown on a farm or in a garden

yield (YEELD) to produce

FOR MORE INFORMATION

Books

Lovejoy, Sharon. *Roots, Shoots, Buckets, and Boots: Gardening Together with Children.* New York: Workman Publishing, 1999.

Morris, Karyn, and Jane Kurisu (illustrator). *The Kids Can Press Jumbo Book of Gardening.* Tonawanda, NY: Kids Can Press, 2000.

Web Sites

Community Learning Network: Gardening for Kids Theme Page
www.cln.org/themes/gardening.html
For links to many gardening resources

The Great Plant Escape
www.urbanext.uiuc.edu/gpe/gpe.html
Learn about plants while playing a fun game

INDEX

ABOUT THE AUTHOR

Cecilia Minden, PhD, is a literacy consultant and the author of many books for children. She is the former director of the Language and Literacy Program at Harvard Graduate School of Education in Cambridge, Massachusetts. She would like to thank fifth-grade math teacher Beth Rottinghaus for her help with the Real World Math Challenges. Cecilia lives with her family in North Carolina.